T0196271

Rambling Observations
of a
Peaceful Mind

Rambling Observations
of a
Peaceful Mind

CHRISTIAN M. BARRACLOUGH

authorHOUSE®

AuthorHouse™
1663 Liberty Drive
Bloomington, IN 47403
www.authorhouse.com
Phone: 1-800-839-8640

First published by AuthorHouse   01/03/2012

ISBN: 978-1-4685-3279-1 (sc)
ISBN: 978-1-4685-3280-7 (hc)
ISBN: 978-1-4685-3281-4 (ebk)

Library of Congress Control Number: 2011963108

Printed in the United States of America

Table of Contents

Without...

Without the shedding of tears
Would wisdom have come
Without the pains brought by change
Would we ever have grown

Without the loneliness of it's absence
Would true love have been known
Without the depths of our sorrows
Would the seeds of joy have been sown

Without the warmth of a safe haven
Would we know the meaning of home
Without the hopelessness of being lost
Would our true selves then be known

Without the hunger pains of that which we lack
Would gratitude then be shown
Without the futility of oppression
Would freedom have been born

Without the helplessness of depression
Would what's important in life ever show
Without the divisions we face
Would we ever become one

Without the contradictions
That surround
Would our true selves
Have been found

Around the Corner

What's around the next corner
Not yet, can you see
The culmination of dreams
Or similar fears
You have seen
What's around the next corner
Depends on what
You believe

Rising Sun

The past belongs to yesterday
This time
Is not like before
Learn the truth
Of the lessons it taught you
No need to look back
Just close the door
The past may have made you
Who you are today
But can not define
Who you will become
Your future has not been written
Find your place
With the rising sun

Dreams Denied

How can you deny
All the dreams left inside
Never brought to the light
In withering darkness they hide
Never given the chance
The wine flows freely
As we dance
Around the distractions
Arousing to the senses
So they are
As they keep us from dreaming
From finding other ways
Passions burn up our nights
And we sleep through our days
As time passes by
We forget to ask why
We just watch all the years
Admiring our collection of fears
Staying content with far less
Than our weakest dreams
Let us possess
Forgotten in darkness
Our dreams die
Never brought to the light
Never having a chance
To be right

Seeing Life

To the stars I looked
As I forswore
As I crossed the troubled waters
Once more

Never again would I let
My fears hem me in
Passing the challenges
Without and within

For life keeps on going
As the world it does spin
Remembering days
Of life full of play
Through seeking, did I explore
What life brought me here for

For fears pass me by
Seeking answers of why
Finding reasons within
As the world it does spin

As the clouds in the sky
Do constantly change
The transformation of my life
Does feel much the same

No need of the worries
As I'm finding my way
Seeing life, through fresh eyes
As a child at play

An Inarguable Fact

My life is what it is
I am, where I'm at
No resisting or complaining
Can change, an inarguable fact

So I'm left with a choice
Since I am only me
Do I let emotions keep me imprisoned
Or do I choose to be free

Do I choose to be happy
Do I choose misery
Do I choose to be burdened
Do I choose to be me
Often overlooked
Though it's simple to see

Regardless, of where I'm at
The choice, is mine alone
An inarguable fact

Just One Dream

The realization of just one dream
Brings inspiration to us all
For it is more than just one dream
It brings validity to them all

For in pursuing just one dream
So many more are carried along
As the beautiful sound of one note
Heralds a symphony of song

As if one is forgotten
Or given up on way too soon
The whole composition feels its loss
A symphony, with one less tune

So much more than just your dream
It is in dreams, we all do share
They are the reasons we keep on living
How we rise above despair

So much more than just one dream
Though only one, or so it seems
For the realization, of them all
Begins...with just one dream

CHRISTIAN M. BARRACLOUGH

Not the Man

I am not the man, you met before
Though surely, I was once
I am not the troubled man you've seen
It was something I had become
I am not the man who was mad at the world
Though that's something, I have done
I am not the man who did you wrong
He was one I fought hard, to overcome
I am not the man who looked down on others
Once I was blind, but now I see
I am not the man who passed judgment on others
Claiming them guilty, instead of me
I am not the man who put chains on all others
Made them slaves, so I'd be free
I am not the man so lost in his vices
Though I walked many years down his road
I am not the man locked away in his crisis
In shame, I walked alone
I am not the same man who lost his way
Though many nights, I had no home
I was not made a man by a career I had chosen
They were only professions, I have done
No actions I've taken, can define who I am
For the truth, I've searched and searched
I've tried to define myself often
By actions I've taken, here on earth
As I peeled back all illusions
The man I thought, I wanted to be
I peeled back all illusions
Until I finally, could clearly see
Past it all
I found only love
Only love...
Yeah...that's me

It's Not...

It's not failure, that kills our spirits
Nor tragedies, nor disasters

It's not the accumulated stress
As the world spins ever faster

It's not the heavy burdens we carry
Or mounting responsibilities we face

It's not the hopelessness of the lost
Or of feeling out of place

It's not the uncertainties ahead
Or regrets we've left behind

It's not the state of our health
Of our bodies and minds

It's not the fears that we live with
And face everyday

It's not the struggles we live through
As we search for our way

All of these have their place
Or so it does seem

The only thing, that kills our spirits
Is the absence...of dreams

The Goal is to Grow

At times life is a lesson
And the soul's goal is to grow
Finding truth and expression
Shining bright to behold

And the journey is sacred
Though at times, it feels less
Through love shared, and love tasted
We find the truth, in life's tests

And tested we are
Though there's no way to fail
We simply get another chance
To see truth, through the veil

As we see, each other as one
As we find ways to help
As we express love, for each other
As we express love, for ourselves

You

So hard it may seem
To just be who you are
To follow your dreams
All in all, that's just the start
It requires saying what you mean
And speaking from the heart
Not following others
Simply playing, your own part
With millions of clones
We would never progress
Never be open to change
And surely fail in life's tests
For what purpose would it serve
If each one changed their direction
And blindly followed along
Never taking time, for introspection
For each person is unique
Each one has something to say
And to drown out just one voice
Is a tragedy. in it's own way
Never let someone dissuade you
It is truly your right to choose
Never rob the world, of the gift that is
Uniquely, exquisitely, You

CHRISTIAN M. BARRACLOUGH

Own Your Life

As we learn and we grow
Through our days and our nights
We finally come to the truth
That we must, own our lives

Not speaking of control
Even though it may seem
For complete control of all aspects
Is an impossible dream

So how is this done
If controls, we do lack
The concept of owning our lives
Is about taking them back

To own one's own life
Means accepting the pain
To weather the storms
Maintain faith through the rain

To own one's own life
Means to carry the weight
To shoulder the burden
To accept our own fate

To own one's own life
Is to accept what we're given
Our shortcomings, our limits
Change what we can, and keep living

RAMBLING OBSERVATIONS OF A PEACEFUL MIND

To own one's own life
Means overcoming the hate
Seeing the similarities in us all
Allowing differences to dissipate

To own one's own life
Means acceptance of change
When met without fear
It gives reason for hope over pain

To own one's own life
Emotions must be understood
Do they mask, or express
Your own highest good

To own one's own life
Is to be mindful how we speak
Do we escalate conflict with our words
Or do we, inspire peace

To own one's own life
Gratitude must be felt
When someone offers their love
When someone offers their help

To own one's own life
Is to learn from our mistakes
To heal the pain that caused them
Free ourselves from returning to that place

CHRISTIAN M. BARRACLOUGH

To own one's own life
We constantly learn and we grow
To accept the pace of that growth
Whether it's fast, or it's slow

To own one's own life
Means it's your life to live
No one can live it for you
No matter how much they give

The decisions are yours
Decisions only you can make
And the results of your choices
Determines the path your life takes

Embrace each challenge with joy
Embrace times, both good and bad
Embrace the highs and the lows
Embrace every moment that we have

It's a beautiful composition
A tapestry woven through time
Own your life every moment
For my friend, it's your life

Endless Abundance

Every morning
I watched the sunrise
As majestic colors
Treated my eyes
And everyday
I walked the seashore
Upon fresh sand
From the ocean floor
And everyday
I collected shells
In endless colors, shapes and sizes
Teaching me one of life's greatest lessons
Endless abundance is found
In life's small surprises

Love is...

Love is priceless
The only thing
In this world
That is
It seeks only to share itself
To never be contained
It can never be taken
But can be received
It can never be lost
But can go unseen
It can never be manipulated
Without inviting pain in
It can not stay apparent
When surrounded in sin
For love has no cost
Can not be bought
Can not be sold
The only gift
In this world
The more you give
The more you hold

Angel Song

Though love is love
One can not deny
The feeling of love
The warm glow lit inside
Though two be but two
Until they seek and then find
The sweet taste of love
As two hearts intertwine
Lifting yet lifting
Upon angel's wings
Two hearts bathed in bliss
Across the heavens
Angels sing

The Key

It's easy
To see problems
Overwhelming at times
But problems are merely
Opportunities
In disguise
A lesson
To be learned
One we try
Not to see
But it always comes back
Until we start
To believe
That we all
Are the same
And forgiveness
Is key

Set Me Free

Breaking free, breaking free
It is about time, I did this for me
After long years of tunnel vision
It is about time I woke up to see
That no one kept me in prison
There was no one else but me
It was clearly my choice to stay locked up
For only I, was holding the key
And now the sky does seem less dark
And the future seems oh so bright
As I give up my addictions, all my self-made afflictions
And open my eyes, accepting the light
And there still will be storms
But I've seen them before
Without fear, I'll embrace every change
For it is about time
That I fully accept my life
And use my key
To set me free

No Limits

Why would you limit yourself
Belittle yourself
Leaving your dreams to die
Was it something they told you
Too harshly did scold you
Exposing fears, that led you to hide
Ignore all the limits
Live your dreams every minute
Radiating the love held inside
Don't go chasing their ways
And go wasting your days
Believing you can not achieve it
Let love flow through your veins
And let joy be maintained
Life is a dream how you live it
Life is a dream love within it
Live your life
As you dream
With no limits

Slip and Stumble

We all slip and stumble
On the rocky roads
That we travel
Weather storms
Of devastation
That lay bare
All we have built
Through the wreckage
We start to see
The best things in life
They never leave
Though at times
May be hidden
Waiting for us
To believe

Love's Doorway Home

The city's lit up
And the parties roll on
No one's asleep
Until well after dawn
I step out in the night
Toward downtown's crowds and bright lights
Feel right at home
In this sea full of strangers
As I walk the fine line
Between excitement and danger
Don't know where this night will take me
Don't know when this will end
No idea if I spent
Last night with demons or friends
But I will try again, and then try once more
One day I'll truly feel home
If I can just
Find the door

Change

All things must change
A simple truth, yet profound
To reaffirm this belief
All one must do, is look around

Or to look at one's self
For changes occur everyday
Resistance is futile
For in this world, it's the only way

Though we search for ways to fight it
To hold on to what we know
Accepting inevitable change as a fact
Is the only sane way to go

Accepting this fact
Can change our perspectives and views
Accepting each occurence
With peace of mind, to calmly choose

For all things are transient
As are times, both good and bad
Being down is only temporary
And know that this too shall pass

Only One

How much fun
Do you have

In times
Good and bad

Can you offer smiles through sorrows
Can you make others laugh

Can you find reasons to be happy
When there's little to cheer

Does your heart radiate
Do you draw others near

Are your trials and tribulations
Put in their proper place

Through lessons we all must learn
Do you help to spread divine grace

And if you really, had a choice
From more than one, could you choose

Only one person to spend an entire lifetime with
My friend, would it, be you

Love is
Within
Never
Without

Excuses

What excuses do you make
When life changes your plans
Do you say I just can't
Or do you say, I still can

Do you seek to find answers
Why things went as they did
Do you seek to place blame
Like it's someone's fault for this

Would that make you happy
That someone was wrong
Would that give you peace
Allowing you to move on

Do you find answers through your anger
Are they clear to see when you're calm
Is there any justification in the perception
That a decision was wrong

Maybe it happened for the best
Though you can't see it now
Sometimes the truth requires patience
And what answers are to be found
In excuses anyhow

False Images

What purpose, serves the lies
Creating images we can't maintain
All they see is our false fronts
Only truth that they know, are our names

And the only face that they know
Are the ones that we show
To accomplish a given end

And how much time then is spent
How many demands must be met
Before we, can call ourselves friends

And upon what can we depend
And which friends are genuine
When the faces must change all the time

What's the use of the games
That we try to maintain
When the truth, must come out in the end

Is it truly so hard
To just be who we are
When there's really no use to pretend

Contradictions

How many contradictions, will it take
Before changes, are clear to make
As children, we are taught to share
When playing games, we are taught to play fair
We are taught,
    Not to lie
    Not to cheat
    Not to steal
We are taught to be aware
Of how we make others feel
We are taught to finish our meals
And never to waste
We are taught to walk through the house
Not to run through in haste
We are taught to treat others
As we'd like to be treated
We are told, it's only a game
When we lose, and feel defeated
We are taught we can accomplish anything
We set our mind to
If we work hard, do as we're told
If we play by the rules
And then we grow up
Or that's what we say
And the lessons we've learned
Became less clear along the way
Now how often do we share
When we have more then we could ever need
Then we give a little back
With tax breaks on charity

RAMBLING OBSERVATIONS OF A PEACEFUL MIND

Now losing is not an option
We play to win at all costs
And somewhere along the way
The idea of fair play has been lost
Today lying, cheating and stealing
Has sadly, become the norm
For that we have speech writers
To tell us how to say, we've been reformed
And being aware of the feelings
Of our sisters and brothers
More important how we feel
Than the feelings of others
And finishing our meals, and never to waste
We build disposable technologies
Every couple of years they are replaced
And about walking slowly
Not running in haste
Even multi-tasking is not enough
For our human race
And playing by the rules
Please excuse me if I laugh
For which leaders, or which organizations
Are up to that task
Is it really a surprise
Our world is in the shape that it's in
When the mantra of the day
Is we play only to win

CHRISTIAN M. BARRACLOUGH

Seems the lessons from pre-school
Are more valuable
Than those we learned in college
We've unlearned the foundation of being human
And we call that, acquiring knowledge

Can we unlearn all this knowledge
Of deceit, hate and vice
And go back to our earlier lessons
Of just, playing nice

Daybreak

Just as day breaks
Following night
So must truth then
Come to light
For there is no
Place to hide
As the darkness
Subsides

CHRISTIAN M. BARRACLOUGH

Torn and Tattered

Time passes by
Years upon years
Torn and tattered
My dreams stayed intact
As if mirrors
Never shattered
But broken they were
In a million pieces
And then
I put them back
One by one
Renewed my faith
Once again

Mere Illusions

Is it more, than mere illusion
Another reason, for more confusion
Or just a cloud, that will pass
Another time, that won't last
Should worry and fear, consume my thoughts
No dear friend, I think not
For I've seen this before
As storms rage, by my door
Mere illusions, or so I feel
Passing too quickly,
To be real

CHRISTIAN M. BARRACLOUGH

True Expression

Why work
A job you don't like
To buy things
You don't need
To achieve success
That remains hollow
To impress people
You don't care for
To suppress creativity
You alone, can create
To achieve status
An abstract concept
Chasing dreams
You didn't dream
Rather than, a life full of meaning
In the expession
Of your heart's true desire

At the Goal

The key to happiness
Is your state of mind
What you carry along
And what you leave far behind

It's your view of the world
Do you see more bad or good
Is all you see negative
Would you change that if you could

It all happens, in small steps
As we walk down this road
All races start at the beginning
Rather than, at the goal

CHRISTIAN M. BARRACLOUGH

Awareness

Of what
Are you aware
Are the small joys of life lost
Left out of focus by your stare
Are they lost in the brightness
Of the city light's glare
When was the last time
You heard a bird's song
Which brought a smile to your lips
When too much of your day had gone wrong
When was the last time
A butterfly fluttered by
And you caught a glimpse of life's grace
With no need to ask why
When was the last time
You truly appreciated
The wind blowing through the trees
Making your stress seem so sedated
How often do you sit and wonder
In our world's digital age
When we are bombarded with information
Without the need to turn a page
How often do you enjoy
Life simply, as it is
A sunrise, a sunset
Nature's unending supply of gifts
Does your life move much too fast
For you to clearly see
How much of life we miss, when unaware
What the gift of life, does truly mean

To Grow...

As we grow
We change forms
To become brighter things
We are not
What we once were
Though sometimes
It may seem
A flower is not the seed
From which it grew
From below
It's natural state
A thing of beauty
Unless it decides
Not to grow

Still Hear Your Words

Every single day
I think of you
Of times gone past
Your words so true
I still hear them now
I know just what you'd say
When problems come calling
You still help me today
Still catch me from falling
As all these years pass
I can still hear your words
I can still hear your laugh
Good times may be brief
Good memories never fade
Long years you've been gone
Still with me today
Just wanted to thank you
Your lessons don't fade
All the wise words that you've said
And the ones
You still say

Juliet

Our dear, sweet Juliet
A beautiful angel
That walked among us
As she always has
Is as she always will
Remain
A beautiful angel
Among us still

CHRISTIAN M. BARRACLOUGH

Depression

Though depression brings with it
Unbearable pain
It also brings truth
That must be ascertained
It magnifies the discontent
Harboring transformative change
To dispel misconceptions
And truly live...once again

Flows With

A river flows with
Not resisting
The terrain
A life lived in harmony
Flows along
Just the same

Power to be Found

Our lives come down to choices
Of that we make each day
And giving those choices to someone else
Only keeps us from our way

Though it's right, at times, to seek council
The final decisions are ours alone
No one else can do it for us
No one else can build our homes

And there are places designed to capture
Our attention, our hearts, our minds
But as the facade breaks down, no soul to be found
Only emptiness, is what we find

And possessions and vices are one in the same
We waste years to just acquire
As they convince us, we can not live without
No matter how strong their hold, in time their truth expires

For the power you hold inside of you
Is the power that brings forth change
And all the distractions about which this world is built
Brings complacency, and more of the same

Your power is a gift that was given you
And in time, you'll understand why
The only power in life to be acquired
Is the power, to be found...inside

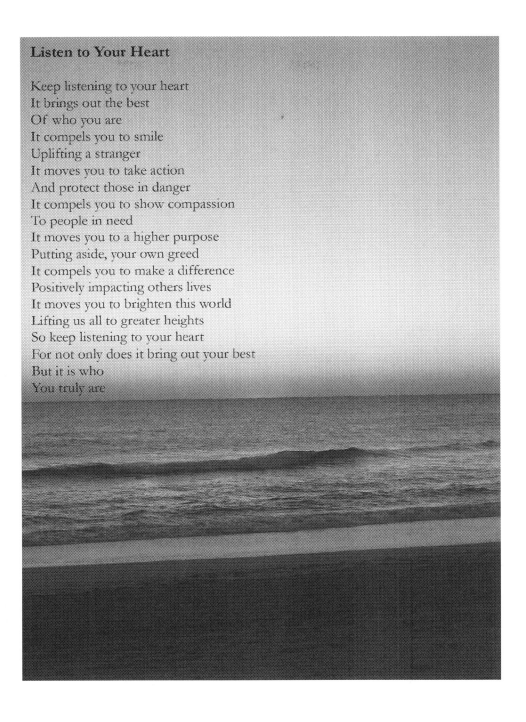

Listen to Your Heart

Keep listening to your heart
It brings out the best
Of who you are
It compels you to smile
Uplifting a stranger
It moves you to take action
And protect those in danger
It compels you to show compassion
To people in need
It moves you to a higher purpose
Putting aside, your own greed
It compels you to make a difference
Positively impacting others lives
It moves you to brighten this world
Lifting us all to greater heights
So keep listening to your heart
For not only does it bring out your best
But it is who
You truly are

CHRISTIAN M. BARRACLOUGH

The Best Things in Life

They say the best things in life are free
So that leaves out the big houses
Cars, and financial security

All can disappear, and their replacement isn't free
I'd much rather have love, peace,
Compassion and tranquility

We must have more things, so we're led to believe
We must buy, and buy more
It's almost like a disease

And while we're working long hours
To make these ends meet
Who suffers the most, it is our families

So what is it you value
What most deserves your time
Does life get the best of you
Or do you, get the best of life

Be Strong Enough

Be strong enough
To handle the silence
Somedays we are meant
To walk alone

Be strong enough
To handle the storms
For somedays
We have no homes

Be strong enough
To handle the changes
For somedays
We are meant to grow

Be strong enough
To carry the burdens
It's how we make
Our lives our own

Be strong enough
To handle the silence
Strong enough to find your way
Yours alone

Through Clouds

Through clouds does the light shine down upon
And alight the morning dew
As I've weathered many cold dark nights
In the hope, that I'd find you
As I've allowed no struggles to hold me back
And mountains I've overcome
In the faith of finally finding
Love's sweet caress
I've traveled, through the fiercest storms
Though again and again I've faced down life's tests
Pruned back, that I may grow
So now may step forth
And give you my best
That we may bask
In love's sweet glow
For my love grew inside
No longer to hide
My heart's love, now I truly know
And I'm ready to find
That sweet love so sublime
Across the world
Lonely hearts do yearn for
Alone I've gone through the years
As I've shedded life's tears
For the truth
My heart held in store
For no measure of fear
No sum of years upon years
Can dissuade me from finding
My taste of Heaven
Sharing the love
I've lived this life for

Play at Life

Look for learning
That holds meaning
Each new experience
As an adventure
Play at life
As a child

Realizations

One day I realized
The best drummer, I would never be
And so, I stopped playing
One day I realized
My frame was too small
The best athlete, I would never be
And so, I stopped playing
One day I realized
The best artist, I would never be
And so, I stopped writing
One day I realized
Many people owned more than me
And so, I devoted all of my time
To earning money
But happiness never came
The best businessman, I would never be
And so, I felt lost
A new direction was needed, for me
And then one day, I found myself
Surrounded by children and their love
Not because, I was the best at anything
For surely, I was not
And then the realization came
It was my love, my laughter
The fun we shared just playing
What game it was, didn't matter
What the score was, was never counted
But the laughter, was immeasurable
The joy and fun, like a forgotten dream
And then that day, I finally realized
What value my life held
What held importance for me
And ever since, I've been playing
Never waking, from this dream

Uncomparable Journey

One soul's journey
Is not comparable
To another's
Each has
His own path
To follow
Lessons to learn
Meaning to find
And dreams
To realize

CHRISTIAN M. BARRACLOUGH

The Pawn

A pawn on a chessboard
Expendable with disdain
Battles rage all around
As we try to maintain
This war between kings
Leave few pawns to remain
Why do we continue to fight
When the results are the same
The way of this world
And they call it...
A game

The Beast

The beast's fangs
Glisten bright
As it prowls
Smiling pride
Invading homes
It devours
Everything
We sought to hide
The pangs of
Hunger never fade
Every night
The same as day
Insatiable to the end
Our defenses, can't defend
How to hunt down the hunter
How to stop the demons inside
Clawing, pulling us under
Giving us nowhere left to hide
Channeling all of our rage
At the one which we fear
Channeling all of our hate
After the beast we give chase
Then the slaughter commences
The evil beast it must die
In our bloodlust and our fury
To the truth we stay blind
For the beast that we killed
In front of us
Now prowls around inside

Kind of Life

What kind of life
Lives a workaholic
What kind of life
Lives an alcoholic
Running from ourselves
The only one, we can't escape
Running from ourselves
We forget to give, we only take
What kind of life
Would we live
If we'd just, change our ways
Would we see
Calmer nights
Would we embrace
Brighter days
The decision, is yours alone
Do you seek
A better way

Good Hearts

Wasting time
Looking for riches
For riches, come and go
Wasting time
Seeking fame
Gone with a word
You'll never know
Nothing is permanent
Life changes everyday
No protection from
The ups and downs
Of life, it is the way
Only thing there is worth finding
Are good hearts
To share your days

CHRISTIAN M. BARRACLOUGH

Grow Up

Grow up just enough
To acquire a few possessions
Grow up just enough
To weather life's slow recessions
Grow up just enough
To put your life's plans in place
But never grow up too much
You lose yourself
In life's race
Never grow up too much
To lose the child within
That reminds us life's fun
When we just play
Not caring
Who wins

As a huge canyon
Cut from stone
Simply by water
In a flowing line
So may insurmountable
Problems be overcome
With adaptable effort
And patient time

A Life Defined

Who are you
Who are you
Is it what's inside
Or what you do

For the answer to this question
Is the root of it all
And can answer most others
Once we've heeded this call

Though it requires introspection
Sometimes a formidable task
Though finding your answer, to this one question
Leaves much less to ask

Looking at what we are not
So much easier to see
Clearing away the misconceptions
Leaves us free to just be

We are not movie characters
Defined lives, by a script
A life modeled on fantasy
No full life, can be defined by this

RAMBLING OBSERVATIONS OF A PEACEFUL MIND

Or the life lived by a music
Or someone's spoken word
Is just following another
Repeating something we've heard

Or the life defined by a profession
Which is just something we do
Simply a means for sustenance
Something we can't always choose

Can it be the sum of our actions
Or things that we have said
But these change everyday
And the past only resides, in our heads

So who are you, who are you
How can you be defined
There is no one word answer
It's how you're living your life

Each day it's your choice
Who you are, who you will be
In a constant state of evolving
No definitions...when you're free

CHRISTIAN M. BARRACLOUGH

Taking Time

We can follow
Another's lead
We can blend
In conformity
We can live
A whole life
Without taking time
To know
Our true selves

With This Moment

With this moment
What will you do
The same things you've done before
Or something, completely new
Will this moment pass you by
In the future to lament
Or will it create an everlasting memory
Allowing your soul to feel content
Will you let this moment slip away
Unconsciously linking it to the past
A road you've traveled too many times
A time that did not last
Will you ignore this moment
As you look beyond
Inconsequential in your path
Too slow today to recognize
For the future is coming fast
Or will you embrace this moment
Of a fresh new day
As a chance to start anew
And break away from common ways
Will this moment bring a breath of fresh air
Filling your sails as you depart
Will it bring you to new paths to travel
Will it increase the love within your heart
With this moment
What will you do
Will you cast all fear aside, and live your life
With this moment
It's up to you

Two Kinds of Love

They say love can be defined in many ways
Though in truth there are but two
And the one you choose to send out to the world
Will be the same that's returned to you

Some say that love is intertwined with pain
Though that's clearly not the case you see
For love and pain are direct opposites
And as you give so shall you receive

The love that causes pain is a selfish love
Much more prevalent in our time
Filled with concepts like ownership
Sometimes yours, but mostly mine

With selfish love, it's a constant struggle
For who has power, who is in control
It constantly runs the same cycles in circles
Winning and losing, and fighting again, until, the cycle gets old

Then we run out to find a new partner
One that thinks the same way as us
Without looking inside, the only thing we will find
Is more of the same, but hidden by lust

And to break past the cycle of selfish love
True love must be found within
For without loving yourself, you can love no one else
And the only love you will find is selfish

And what is true love, it is love unconditional
And it truly emanates from your soul
No need, for judging or fighting
Or finding ways to manipulate for control

It's about treating another as you'd like to be treated
No expectations of a pre-conceived role
It's the love unconditional that warms all around us
It is the love that makes us all whole

And by clearly understanding
Makes it easy to see, which one is in your midst
There's no reason for pain as the selfish try to gain
For you deserve a better love than this

A selfish love, or love unconditional
In which love do you believe
For the love you choose to send out to the world
Is the love, you deserve to receive

CHRISTIAN M. BARRACLOUGH

Why Are We Here

Why are we here
Of themselves, each one must ask
A question haunting man since the beginning of time
Taking each religion to task

At the heart of every philosophy
This question does exist
Man's unending quest for the meaning of life
A simple answer for the complexity of all this

Each one must find his own answers
Each one must find his key
Unlocking the mysteries of his path
Amid myriad ways to eternity

And no path can be wrong
If the destination is home
And what would we have learned
If we never had to walk alone

And what would be the point
If we all traveled down the same line
With no mysteries to discern
Life would amount to a prison term
Everyone just doing their time

RAMBLING OBSERVATIONS OF A PEACEFUL MIND

Do you really believe
Life is only what we see
That there is not much more
Beyond the illusions of scenes

For what sense would it make
That we are only here to consume
It's time we saw through the illusions
And allow seeking answers to resume

For we are destroying our world
And destroying ourselves
Living lives unexamined
And creating our own hell

Though arguments rage unending
Seems to be no easy way
The truth that changes are necessary
Is clear to all, as plain as day

Are we more than just parasites
Sucking the Earth dry
Can we not live in harmony
Establishing better lives

CHRISTIAN M. BARRACLOUGH

The Brink of Change

As life drifts and floats on by
I always come back to the question of why
Why so overwhelming, why is that how it seems
While most walk around, oblivious like a dream
Why does the big picture, seem so clear to me
But lays obscured to most others
Like they can't or won't see
As we run around in circles
Different circumstances, yet the same
Not paying heed to the consequences
Different choices, same mistakes
Why won't we stand up for change
Why would we accept how things are
Destroying ourselves and the environment
Poor choices, allowed unchallenged for much too long
It can not all be healed in a day
For the polluting took much longer
Once we decide as one to demand change
Our voice will be heard then much stronger
On the verge of, this new era
Why hesitate, to step forth
The fate of our world lies here before us
Why hesitate now, to step forth

Contemplate

My time will be my time
Never before, never after
As I roll along with this flow
Accepting change, because I have to

As hard as it may be
Awaiting the culmination to come
It's all one can do
As another day's done

But the sweet taste ahead
As dreams culminate
Outweighs a thousand dreary days
I contemplate,
As I wait

CHRISTIAN M. BARRACLOUGH

Unbeknownst

How have I persevered
Through hard times, so severe
How have I been able to hold on
When so much had gone wrong
It's unbeknownst to me

What's the point of it all
Times to rise, times to fall
Where did the strength come within
To make it through once again
It's unbeknownst to me

Though at times I've felt lost
And I've truly paid the cost
I know there's a reason I'm still here
A reason I've found the strength, to persevere
Even though, it's unbeknownst to me

Though there is a Divine plan
One I don't understand
And that's just fine you see
Even though it may be
Unbeknownst to me

Shining Brightly

No one can save you
You must save yourself
You're not abandoning others
The only way you can help
Is by forging your path
And shining your light
It is not for you
To drag others
That would rather stay blind
Walk alone if you must
Walking along
Is for them to decide
Just continue
Following your heart
And continue
Shining brightly
Your light

CHRISTIAN M. BARRACLOUGH

Love and Understanding

What have you learned in this life
What can you share and teach others
How many lessons have we learned
Crossing one mountain after another

The inherent value in a life
Measured by troubles overcome
Past the hardships we've faced
We share understanding and love

That's what binds us together
Multiple common threads
Same struggles and tribulations
Same needs and wants to be fed

For we all are the same
As we look past the illusions
Some seek to divide us apart
Though we must forgive their intrusions

For life is about love
Nothing else holds much value
Those missing this point
Remain hollow and shallow

RAMBLING OBSERVATIONS OF A PEACEFUL MIND

Expressing love feeds the soul
Lifting us all so much higher
To our own highest good
To what else, could we aspire

To share love and understanding
Sown seeds now have grown
Choosing to share wisdom with others
Showing each soul, their life to own

CHRISTIAN M. BARRACLOUGH

For Ourselves or For Others

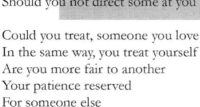

Is the love, we have for another
The same we have for ourselves
Are we critical of those we love
Are we much harder on ourselves

Is forgiveness, only for others
Do we not deserve the same too
Is compassion reserved
For a special someone
Should you not direct some at you

Could you treat, someone you love
In the same way, you treat yourself
Are you more fair to another
Your patience reserved
For someone else

For the love held within
Must be directed both ways
If we are ever
To find the balance
Of true love's
Sweet embrace

A Glimpse of the Infinite

Lost in thought and time
Upon the beach I sit
And comes to me in form of rhyme
A glimpse, of the infinte
As I calmly watch the ebb and flow
Of the ocean's unending tide
I see with insight how the energy goes
Around us on all sides
As I watch the waves rush forth
Then slowly they roll back
I am reminded there is so much
In life, that's just like that
Each new day is born
But must give way to the night
Each one has it's time
But can't claim all, as it's right
Through Winter life rests
Transformations in the Fall
Celebrations through the Summer
While Spring brings growth for us all
There's no slowing of the tide
As the cycle must progress
A process to be remembered
When we seek to resist, a life test
As the energy must flow forth
At times it must recede
So too, we face hardships
Intermingled with our dreams
All energy flows in it's natural ways
A perfect plan, such as this
Only a moment can we see, the perfect complexity
In a glimpse, of the infinite

CHRISTIAN M. BARRACLOUGH

The Dream Inside

How does it look
The dream held deep inside
Is it similar, to the life you lead
Or is it one, you must find

Could you be, content with less
Blaming the circumstances, of your life
Is that a truth, that makes you content
Or a fear, behind which you hide

Would life be complete
Never having tried
Can you live a full life
Knowing you let your dreams die

For what have you to lose
Justifying, unconscious fears
For a life left unlived
Is just a wasting of years

One must retrieve their own spirit
From the lies that were told
From the untruths, we believed
From the fears, we let take hold

For no one would know better
Than what your life means to you
Fear can only hold you back, if you let it
For it is your life...to choose

This Time

Why couldn't it be, this time
Past the charades
All the superficial ways
Why couldn't it be, this time

Why couldn't there be
A time reserved just for me
When things went just right
Positive changes in life
Why couldn't it be, this time

Long days and long nights
Of a past now forgotten
Of times, that can't hold me down
Soon my time, will come around
Why couldn't it be, this time

My prayers have gone out
Have no time, left for doubt
Miracles do happen
In their own time, their own actions
Why couldn't it be, this time

There's no reason it couldn't
No reason it shouldn't
Why it couldn't be mine
Why it shouldn't be mine
Why couldn't it be, this time

CHRISTIAN M. BARRACLOUGH

A Thought I Think

Is what I have thought
What I truly think?
Or was I told
To think
That which I have thought?
I think I'll think
My own thoughts
And leave them
To their thoughts
To think
What they will

Deep Longings

Follow, my dear
The deep longings of your soul
Though they run contrary
To the whims
Of the world around you

Be not pulled into their ways
For their ways
Deny the truth
Of who you are

Rise above
To your true expression
And lift up those
Who can see and hear

Condemn not the rest
But bless them
Silently in your heart
For they seek the path
As you do
But know it not

Follow, my dear
The deep longings of your soul
They hold the truth
Of who you are

Inspirations of a Moonlit Sky

As I gaze, upon the moonlit sky
Unending questions, go streaming by
Asking why, asking why
Pondering life, as it unfolds
Unending questions, go streaming by
All with answers,
As yet, untold...

And as my eyes drift
From bright star, to bright star
My thoughts go flying far
Above all my troubles
My pain left behind
Above all my fears
My emotions, not blind

And as my soul, then visits the Heavens
Surrounding blessings do unfold
Unremembered bliss, at all the wonders
The uncomparable love, left to behold

And as my soul, comes drifting down
Past the Heavens, through the stars
I carry that love back down with me
Swelling the limits of my heart

And as my eyes fall back upon my reality
Must finds ways to share
That love so pure
Amidst the minefield, in front of me

And as I gaze, upon the moonlit sky
Unending questions, go streaming by
But the questions of why
No longer stream by
They are only of how
How...do I make things right

CHRISTIAN M. BARRACLOUGH

The Couple

His shiny car is long gone
In a yard, collecting rust
Her jewelry and diamonds now rest
In a box, collecting dust

His muscles are weaker
Not as impressive to see
Her fancy dresses in the closet
Became threadbare, eventually

This life they have shared
Began with excitement and dreams
Pain and disappointment, they have weathered
But you can easily see

The love in their eyes
That was there from the start
As all else has faded
Except the love, in their hearts

Wings to Fly

Does the caterpillar lament
That she has no wings
Does she give in to despair
Cause she has yet to fly, yet to sing
Does she search the world over
To learn how to grow
Is it a knowledge to be found
Or an intrinsic wisdom, she knows
Does she search wide and far
To find colors to spin
Does she find them buried deep
When she decides, to look within

Or does she grow right away
Knowing only one, or two hues
Does she then, only one perspective
The world, through only one view
Does she know more than one dimension
A multi-dimensional being
Does know, but not how
Does she see, without seeing
Does she know deep inside
When it's time to withdraw
It's time for healing and growth
When it's time to live on

For there will be no wings,
Of brilliant colors
Unless she takes time to grow
And takes the time, to look within
Herself...to know

Anticipation

Sometimes the waiting
Is just what we need
Though it's not always
So easily seen

But in the building anticipation
Heightens the desire
Surrounding your dream

For enacted in haste
Only brings more mistakes
Without the time
To learn from the last

The anticipation
Gives time for reflection
Of the momentum
That builds through the past

So accept now this wait
And give thanks for this day
And seek peace
In contemplation
Of a life-long
Anticipation
For your sweetest dreams
Culmination

Illusion of Time

Some live in the past
Some live for tomorrow
Living in times, that don't exist
Can bring nothing but sorrow

For we can not rewind
To live in a day that is done
No way to go back
No holding back, the rising sun

For the past, is already gone
And tomorrow, it never comes

Tomorrow is an illusion
For as it draws near
We're left with today
And tomorrow disappears

All we have is today
What will we do
What will we say

Only illusions
The past and future
Only time we live
Is today

CHRISTIAN M. BARRACLOUGH

Tomorrow Today

Tomorrow, today
Sometimes it's all the same
It will wait, it will wait

If today's not the day
Then when, will it be
Will tomorrow feel different
With what guarantee

For they both are the same
Only today, brings forth change

If tomorrow's the day
Then change, will have to wait
And how long, you can't tell
And no decision is made

If change, is what you need
The only way it will be
With no time left to wait
What you've waited for...
Is today

All the Same

Do you seek happiness in this life
Does not your neighbor as well
Do you yearn to find love
Does not a stranger as well
Do you seek to be comforted
And safe from the storm
Does not everyone else
No matter their face or their form
Do you seek to have abundance
Of the finer things in life
Does not everyone else
Seek the same things in time
Do you seek to be loved
And to love those around you
Does not everyone else
Seek to find that same love too
Do you seek to know God
Of a true understanding
Does not everyone else
Religious differences notwithstanding
Does it make sense some should have
While others should not
That we should fight for what we have
Because that's what we were taught
Can you see the possibilities
A new perspective would bring
For why should we have
So many divisions
When we all want
The same things

CHRISTIAN M. BARRACLOUGH

The Fool

And though I've spent
So little time
Speaking my heart
Instead of my mind

Playing the statistics
Of clouded logic
From the depths of my soul
Unspoken knowledge

Convincing myself
I'm playing it safe
Convincing myself
There's no other way

Talking myself
Right out of my dreams
For the odds are
Not easily deceived

Much too smart
To take a risk
As it passes me by
Another chance missed

Seems it just isn't smart
To risk your life on a wish
So you may call me a fool
For I'll live my life now...foolish

Cycles of Life

On death and rebirth
And the cycles of life
And though avoidance we try
From the truth, we can't hide

It's when all else is lost
The change slowly begins
Much slower all around
For it begins from within

And the person you were
The way you lived, and held dear
No longer seems to fit
And to faith you draw near

For the world now looks different
And you can't stay the same
Can't look at life the same way
As your soul heralds change

As we know not where to go
But must leap forth in faith
And the trials in place
Unjust as they are
Clarify your truest self
Seen by this world by far

But your growth stops not there
Again the cycle will commence
And clarify you once again
And bring forth, your very best

And again and again
As many times as it takes
For your true self to be shown
To see the value
Your life makes

Obstacles of Change

When the obstacles come
First thing we pray for is change
We think God doesn't listen
For He brings more of the same

Everyday the same old story
Same problems, again and again
And no deliverance from pain
Praying more and more, for change

With the same painful situations
We tend to think, again, why me
With the same oppressive situations
No relief, we can scarcely breathe

Seems we need, a new perspective
Rising above the misconceptions
To finally embrace, a new direction

The first step, is to accept
Not rail against, the problems we face

For denial, does nothing
But prolong all the pain
Viewing ourselves as victims, does nothing
But bring more of the same

When we can accept what we've lost
We feel the first easement of pain
The first chance to breathe, the first break in the rain

The next step is to adapt
To situations we find ourselves in
To find ways to move, to find ways to begin

RAMBLING OBSERVATIONS OF A PEACEFUL MIND

We then start to take solace
In all the little things
And receive a small taste
Of that which hope brings

We can then see, a small glimmer
Of a true, understanding
A small glimpse, of the bigger picture
Of the patterns, we've been withstanding

Moving then to introspection
Of our ideas, and our beliefs
As it begins to make sense
We slowly feel some relief

And as we replace our misconceptions
New ideas emerge to see
The same cycles, need not be repeated
And we once again, begin to believe

Then we can move, to the final stages
Of what we prayed for, all along
We can see, the break in the clouds
Feel the soul, within the song

As we see, it serves no purpose
Running again, into the wall
That could never bring forth change
Just more of the same, my dear, that's all

It never happens that way
Change happens not, from the outside in
Change must take root, and then grow
Flowering out...from within

Back Into the Fire

Back into the fire
Seems that's where I must go
Thought I got past, the past behind me
Learned the lessons, that it showed

But there still, must be a remnant
Linking me to, that former pain
Holding me back, from moving forward
Time to dive in, once again

For though I am, at peace with it
A monumental step that is
A monumental, step toward healing
And the next step to take is this

RAMBLING OBSERVATIONS OF A PEACEFUL MIND

To dig to the root
Behind the misconception
The lies I believed
To get me through

Diving in to introspection
For time alone
Won't heal all wounds

Some false belief
I held as truth
Some false belief
To get me through

Now colors, my waking life
In unconsciousness
Is where it hides

So into the fire, again I go
Finding misconceptions
I let take hold

Digging them up
Bringing them to the light
For in the light
Darkness can't hide

Bringing the lies, into the light
And finally, saying goodbye
To that cold
Dark night

CHRISTIAN M. BARRACLOUGH

Prone to Wander

And though I'm prone to wander
As the days grow ever longer
As I sit and ponder
The design of a plan so intricate
For answers, my logic falters

And so I continue searching
For a clue
That yields the secret
Of this journey I've embarked upon
But know not where it ends

As such I must keep wandering
Toward an encounter
So enchanting
Of the likes
I've never known before

Which raises up the query
Of which I have not a theory
Where my life will then turn
My passions ignite
And then burn

RAMBLING OBSERVATIONS OF A PEACEFUL MIND

And as I truly awake
No more diversions,
Are there to take

Will I still, be prone to wander
For I know in truth much stronger
There's no reason any longer
To search far and wide
For answers
That can only be found
Inside

CHRISTIAN M. BARRACLOUGH

Quiet Calling

Is today what we've dreamed
Or just filled, with possible things
Are we just getting by
Could it be more, if we tried
Are we waiting for change
Things we do, still the same
Holding out here for luck
While the same moves
Keep us stuck
Will we accept how things are
Without the courage, to start
Or is it just time to try
And let failure be damned
Just give it our best
Clarify our beliefs, take a stand
With no fear of falling
And follow our soul's...quiet calling

Returning Thoughts

The shining moon, in the skies
Brings clarity, to my eyes
Lost and found, in my stare
Of my thoughts, unaware
Holding transfixed, in my gaze
Sharing a glimpse, of better days
Clouds drift by, as in a dream
People pass by, like shadows unseen
Wondering what, this night will bring
As my soul deep inside
Begins to sing
Catching a glimpse, of divine truth
Seems I've seen it before
In forgotten youth
As the moon shines, up above
Returning my thoughts now
To love

A Seed in the Breeze

As a seed
We drift
Along with the breeze
Never knowing
Where we'll land

Into the dirt
Another pile of earth
Never knowing
Where we'll stand

The wind carries us on
Thrown about
In the storm
No safe haven
To call a home

The heavy rains
Then pour down
No wind stirring 'round
Encouraging us to then grow

The first few seasons are tough
Our branches tender and young
And we bend
From the pressures around

With nowhere left to run
The harsh realities will come
And we must face
Each one in turn

And as the seasons pass
We grow stronger
Than the last
As we are forced
To adapt and to learn

With each season
We grow taller
The harsh realities
Grow smaller
As we rise above them all

The winds still blow
From east to west
Yet they move us
Less and less
The heavy rains
Only feed our growth

Inhibited, no, not the least
We branch out now
How we please
With strong roots
Grounded back
To our souls

Scarcely possible, to believe
That this towering
Magnificent tree
Was once
A lonely seed
Thrown around
By just a breeze

Christian Michael Barraclough was born and raised, and currently resides in South Florida. No need to list schools attended, professions performed, or accomplishments and failures. For that would not explain who I am anymore than the picture above. Instead, I'll leave you with this.

As our souls then begin
To soar on high, like the wind
Above the struggles, of our minds
That we all work through, in time
Above the physical constrictions
Our bodies endure, in their prisons
A new perspective, our souls see
From on high, all at once
Time to dive in again
For our new lives, have begun